FROM SEA to SHINING SEA

IDAHO

AMY MILLER

Consultants

MELISSA N. MATUSEVICH, PH.D.

Curriculum and Instruction Specialist
Blacksburg, Virginia

IRMA ANDERL

Children's Services
Hayden Public Library
Hayden, Idaho

MARYLYN KALTENECKER

Media Specialist
Middleton Heights Elementary Library
Middleton, Idaho

CHILDREN'S PRESS®

A DIVISION OF SCHOLASTIC INC.

New York • Toronto • London • Auckland • Sydney • Mexico City
New Delhi • Hong Kong • Danbury, Connecticut

Idaho is a Rocky Mountain state.
It is bordered by Montana,
Wyoming, Utah, Nevada, Oregon,
Washington, and British Columbia.

The photograph on the front cover shows shows the capital city of Boise in front of the Boise Foothills.

Project Editor: Meredith DeSousa
Art Director: Marie O'Neill
Photo Researcher: Marybeth Kavanagh
Design: Robin West, Ox and Company, Inc.
Page 6 map and recipe art: Susan Hunt Yule
All other maps: XNR Productions, Inc.

Library of Congress Cataloging-in-Publication Data

Miller, Amy.
    Idaho / Amy Miller.
      p. cm. – (From sea to shining sea)
    Includes bibliographical references (p.) and index.
Contents: Introducing the Gem State—The land of Idaho—Idaho through history—
Governing Idaho — The people and places of Idaho.
  ISBN 0-516-22391-7
  1. Idaho—Juvenile literature. [1. Idaho.] I. Title. II. Series.

F746.3 .M55 2003
979.6—dc21   2002015253

CHILDREN'S PRESS and associated logos are trademarks and or registered trademarks of Scholastic Library Publishing. SCHOLASTIC and associated logos are
trademarks and or registered trademarks of Scholastic Inc.
1 2 3 4 5 6 7 8 9 10 R 12 11 10 09 08 07 06 05 04 03

TABLE of CONTENTS

CHAPTER ONE

INTRODUCING THE GEM STATE

A man fishes for trout amid the quiet beauty of the Snake River.

Idaho is a great place for people who love the outdoors. Hikers and mountain climbers can explore some of the most rugged mountains in the country, such as the Bighorn Crags and the Sawtooth Range. They can also see one of the most spectacular waterfalls in the world, Shoshone Falls. Fishermen and water-skiers enjoy Idaho's Coeur d'Alene Lake, one of the most beautiful lakes in the world.

For thousands of years, Native Americans had Idaho's natural beauty all to themselves. In 1805, Lewis and Clark became the first American settlers to explore the region. Soon after their arrival, fur traders, missionaries, and miners from all around the world began moving to Idaho.

Today, Idaho still attracts many people, and for good reason. The state is famous for the delicious food grown there. Idaho farmers grow more potatoes than any other state. They also grow plenty of barley, sugar beets, and plums. There's also a wealth of mineral resources in

Idaho. Gold, silver, and precious gems, such as garnets, are mined there. Because so many gems are mined in Idaho, it is nicknamed the Gem State.

What else comes to mind when you think of Idaho?

- Proud Native Americans riding the plains on horseback
- Sacagawea helping Lewis and Clark explore an unknown wilderness
- Rugged pioneers traveling the Oregon Trail
- Gold diggers hoping to strike it rich in the late 1800s
- Skiers taking on the slopes at Sun Valley, one of the country's largest ski resorts
- Astronauts training at Craters of the Moon National Monument
- People and animals enjoying millions of acres of protected wilderness land
- The wild Salmon River winding through a dry plain

Idaho means many things to many people. In this book, you'll read about some of the people and places that have helped to develop the Gem State. You'll discover the story of Idaho!

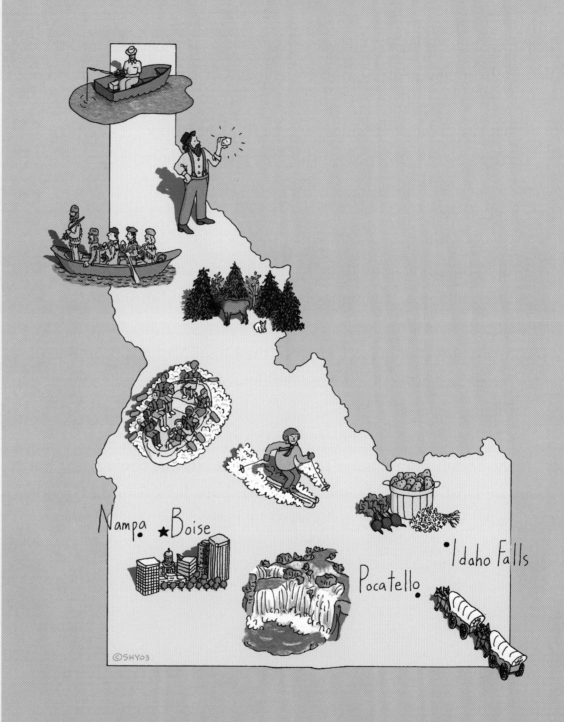

Nampa • ★Boise

Pocatello •

• Idaho Falls

©SHY03

CHAPTER TWO

THE LAND OF IDAHO

If you look at a map, you'll see that Idaho is a Rocky Mountain state in the northwestern part of the United States. It covers 83,574 square miles (216,456 square kilometers). That's an area bigger than all six New England states (Maine, Massachusetts, Rhode Island, Connecticut, New Hampshire, and Vermont), plus New Jersey, Maryland, and Delaware.

The Bitterroot and Beaverhead Mountains form Idaho's northeastern boundary with Montana. Wyoming lies to the east, along with a small slice of Yellowstone National Park. Idaho's western boundary with Oregon and Washington follows the Snake River for hundreds of miles. Nevada and Utah lie to the south, while Canada forms the state's northern border.

More than six hundred million years ago, a shallow sea covered what is now Idaho. Over time, the sea slowly evaporated into a soft, muddy

Coeur d'Alene Lake is one of the most scenic and recreational lakes in Idaho.

The Sawtooth Mountains create a dramatic backdrop for the small town of Stanley.

marshland. About sixty-four million years ago, volcanoes and earthquakes helped create the rugged Rocky Mountains, Idaho's largest land region. South of the Rockies lie Idaho's two other land regions: the Columbia Plateau, and the Basin and Range (sometimes called the Great Basin).

THE ROCKY MOUNTAINS

On a map, you'll see that the northern part of Idaho looks like the handle of a pan turned sideways. This area between Montana and Washington is called the Panhandle. During the Ice Age, glaciers, or thick sheets of ice, carved out deep lakes in the Panhandle, such as Lake Pend Oreille.

The Rocky Mountains begin in the Panhandle and stretch all the way through central Idaho. Many people call central Idaho the Central Wilderness because there are so many steep mountains and deep canyons that few people live there. Some twenty mountain ranges can be found there, including the Bitterroot, Sawtooth, Clearwater, and Salmon River mountains. The highest mountain peaks are located in south central Idaho. Borah Peak, at a towering 12,662 feet (3,859 meters), is the state's highest mountain.

Many people attempt to climb to the top of Borah Peak.

The Rockies provide an abundance of natural resources. More than seventy-two types of precious and semiprecious stones, such as garnets, are mined in the Gem State. Miners also dig for metals such as silver, lead, zinc, gold, and copper, although many mines have closed in recent years.

Timber from the mountains' thick forests is the most abundant and important natural resource produced from the Rockies. Douglas firs, white firs, and spruces are the only trees strong enough to survive in the higher elevations. The largest stand of white pines in America can be found about 75 miles (121 kilometers) northeast of Orofino.

In the lower elevations, hardwood trees, such as birch, cottonwood, and maple thrive. Shrubs such as dogwood, huckleberry, elderberry, and purple heather also grow there. In the spring and summer months, wild-

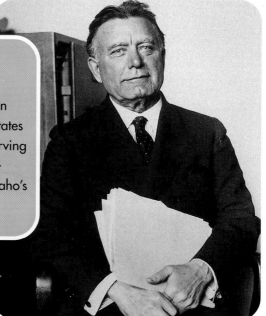

Wildflowers blanket a field in Sawtooth National Recreation Area.

flowers such as the buttercup, lily, and violet blanket Idaho's mountains and valleys. The syringa is the state flower.

Many different kinds of animals make their homes in the Rockies. Sturdy goats and bighorn sheep live in the highest elevations. Bears, deer, elk, mountain lions, squirrels, and other small animals roam the

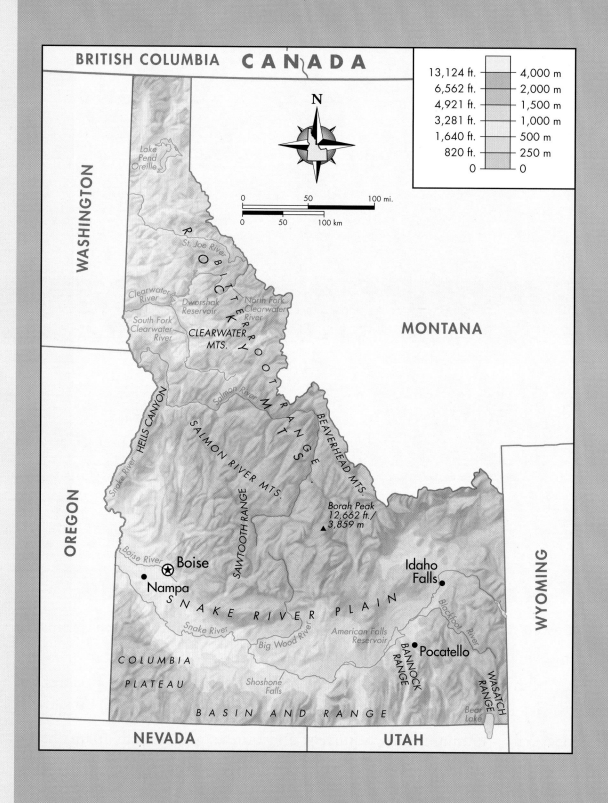

BRITISH COLUMBIA **C A N A D A**

WASHINGTON

MONTANA

OREGON

WYOMING

13,124 ft. — 4,000 m
6,562 ft. — 2,000 m
4,921 ft. — 1,500 m
3,281 ft. — 1,000 m
1,640 ft. — 500 m
820 ft. — 250 m
0 — 0

0   50   100 mi.

0   50   100 km

N

Lake Pend Oreille

St. Joe River

R O C K Y   M O U N T A I N S

B I T T E R R O O T   R A N G E

Clearwater River

Dworshak Reservoir

North Fork Clearwater River

South Fork Clearwater River

CLEARWATER MTS.

Salmon River

HELLS CANYON

SALMON RIVER MTS.

BEAVERHEAD MTS.

SAWTOOTH RANGE

Snake River

Borah Peak 12,662 ft./ 3,859 m ▲

Boise River

★ Boise

● Nampa

S N A K E   R I V E R   P L A I N

Snake River

Big Wood River

American Falls Reservoir

Idaho Falls ●

Blackfoot River

● Pocatello

BANNOCK RANGE

WASATCH RANGE

Bear Lake

COLUMBIA PLATEAU

Shoshone Falls

B A S I N   A N D   R A N G E

NEVADA

UTAH

Elk are a common sight in the Rocky Mountains.

mountain slopes. Gray wolves, which disappeared from Idaho in the early 1900s, were reintroduced to the Frank Church-River of No Return Wilderness Reserve in 1995. Today, between sixty and seventy wolves live on the reserve.

COLUMBIA PLATEAU

Idaho's second-largest land region is the Columbia Plateau. A plateau is a high, level piece of land. The Columbia Plateau follows the Snake River across southern Idaho. Some people in Idaho also call this region the Snake River Plain.

FIND OUT MORE

Compared to the Appalachian Mountains—the principal mountain system of the eastern United States—the Rocky Mountains are young. They were created just 64 million years ago, while the Appalachian Mountains formed about 300 million years ago. During which geologic eras were these mountain ranges formed?

13

Thousands of years ago, lava that erupted through cracks in the Earth created the plateau. Some of the ancient lava flows and craters can still be seen at the 83-square-mile (215-sq-km) Craters of the Moon National Monument, located east of Boise. Visitors can explore volcanic cones and various types of lava flows on this volcanic terrain. The lava flows range in age from 15,000 years to 2,000 years. A variety of wildlife lives in this area, including unusual mammals such as the Great Basin pocket mouse and the yellow-pine chipmunk.

Thousands of years ago, lava eruptions created the unique landscape of Craters of the Moon National Monument.

Today, hundreds of mineral springs created thousands of years ago still bubble up from the ground. A spring is water that flows out of the ground as a small stream or pool. Springs can be either hot or cold. The most famous hot springs in Idaho are Big Creek Springs in Lemhi County, Bald Mountain Springs in Ketchum, and Warm Springs in Boise. The statehouse in Boise and many other buildings in the city are heated from these underground hot springs.

During the Ice Age, animals such as saber-toothed tigers, woolly mammoths, camels, and zebra-like horses roamed the plateau in the marshes along lakes and rivers. You can see the fossils, or preserved remains, of these animals at the Hagerman Fossil Beds National Monument.

Today, many different types of animals still live along the plateau. Large mammals such as elk, moose, antelope, and deer wander the forests. Farmers also graze sheep there. Raccoons, otters, mink, rabbits, foxes, skunks, and squirrels live along rivers and streams. Along the Boise River, beavers cut down trees with their teeth to make dams.

The plateau is also a birdwatcher's paradise. The Snake River Birds of Prey National Conservation Area near Boise has more than eight hundred nesting pairs of raptors, or birds of prey. These include eagles, hawks, falcons, and owls. A large group of white pelicans have lived along the Middle Snake River year-round since the mid-1980s. Migratory birds, such as ducks, egrets, herons, and swans, often stop to rest in Idaho on their annual journey across the United States.

Along the Snake River Plain, the soil is fertile and rich. Many different foods are grown there. Farmers harvest potatoes, beans, sugar beets,

The Snake River Plain is an area of fertile farmland.

peas, fruits, and other crops. Cattle and sheep graze in dry southwestern Idaho.

THE BASIN AND RANGE

The Basin and Range, or the Great Basin, is Idaho's smallest land region. It lies southeast of the Columbia Plateau. It is a narrow strip of lakes, rolling valleys, and grass-covered hills. Some people call this region the Southern Mountains because it includes the Wasatch and Bannock ranges.

Most of the basin is used for grazing cattle and sheep, but it is also home to Bear Lake. Limestone particles and other minerals give Bear Lake a deep blue color. Rare fish, such as the Bonneville cisco, swim there. When Bear Lake freezes, fishermen dig holes in the ice and try to catch these sardinelike fish. Geese, cranes, pelicans, and many species of duck live in the Bear Lake National Wildlife Refuge.

FIND OUT MORE

Millions of years ago, a huge inland sea named Lake Bonneville covered the Great Basin. It stretched across 20,000 square miles (51,800 sq km) of southeastern Idaho, western Utah, and eastern Nevada. Trace an outline of the lake as it once was on a map of the United States. Then draw a picture of or write about the plants and animals that lived in and around the lake.

LAKES, RIVERS, AND WATERFALLS

Idaho has more than two thousand lakes. During the Ice Age, giant glaciers carved out many of these lakes, such as Lake Pend Oreille near the Canadian border. It is more than 2,500 feet (762 m) deep. It is so deep that the United States Navy operates a top-secret testing facility for submarines there.

Idaho's rivers carry more water than the rivers of any other state in

Pend Oreille is the state's largest lake.

the country. The most important river in Idaho is the 1,038-mile (1,671-km) Snake River. It begins in Wyoming and flows westward across southern Idaho through deep canyons, such as Hells Canyon, the deepest gorge in North America. The river makes its way to Washington across spectacular waterfalls, including Shoshone Falls. The falls drops more than 212 feet (65 m)—that's higher than Niagara Falls, located on the border of the eastern United States and Canada.

Fourteen dams along the Snake River turn its mighty current into electricity that people can use. Power created by the dams is so important that half the state's population lives within at least 50 miles (80 km) of the Snake River's banks.

Thousands of tourists come to view Shoshone Falls, the highest waterfall on the Snake River.

Many tributaries, or branches, flow into the Snake River, such as the Clearwater, Big Wood, Blackfoot, and Boise rivers. The Snake River's main tributary is the 420-mile (676-km) Salmon River, which flows west from the Bitterroot Mountains to Oregon. Early explorers called it the "River of No Return" because its rapids were so fierce that many people who dared to travel it never returned.

A rafter approaches fierce rapids on the Salmon River.

FIND OUT MORE

Many years ago, thousands of salmon swam in Idaho's Salmon River. Today, there are very few salmon, even though the Endangered Species Act protects them. That's because dams prevent the salmon from swimming upstream to lay their eggs. What groups are working to save the salmon? How do they want to save them?

With so many rivers and streams, there are plenty of fish in Idaho. Chinook and kokanee salmon, pike, and trout swim the big lakes of Idaho's Panhandle. There's also trout, perch, crappie, and bluegill.

CLIMATE

The climate varies throughout Idaho because of the Rocky Mountains. The mountains in eastern Idaho keep out cold winds from Montana and Wyoming during the winter. The average winter temperature in Boise is 30° Fahrenheit (–1° Celsius). High in Idaho's northern mountains, it gets much colder. On January 18, 1943, the temperature dropped to a freezing –60° F (–51° C) at Island Park Dam.

During summer, winds from the Pacific Ocean keep northern Idaho cooler and wetter than southern Idaho. About 40 inches (102 centimeters) of rain and about 60 inches (152 cm) of snow fall in northern Idaho every year. Some mountain areas get as much as 30 feet (9.1 m) of snow per year.

In southern Idaho, less than 10 inches (25 cm) of rain falls each year, and in the summer it becomes dry like a desert. August is a dangerous time for forest fires. But all of Idaho can become hot and dry. On July 28, 1934, the temperature reached a record 118° F (48° C) in the northern community of Orofino.

Snow blankets a forest of Douglas fir trees.

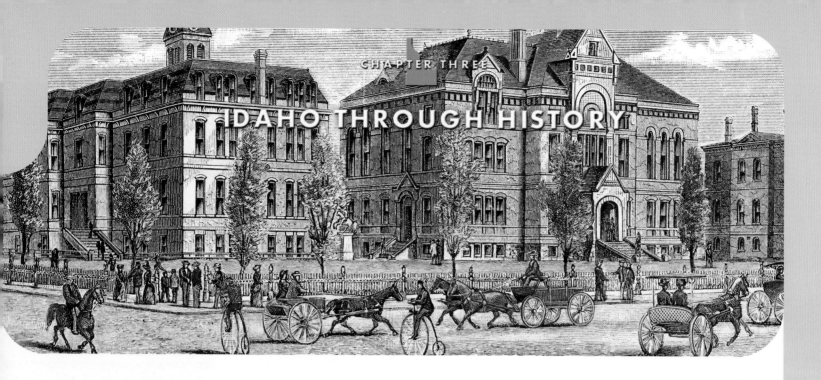

CHAPTER THREE

IDAHO THROUGH HISTORY

This illustration shows a view of Capitol Square in Boise around 1890.

Scientists believe that humans have lived in what is now Idaho for more than 10,000 years. Over time, two major groups of native people emerged in Idaho, but they were separated by the Rocky Mountains. Idaho's northern Panhandle was home to the Nez Percé, the largest tribe in the region. French explorers gave them this name, which means "pierced nose." Although neighboring tribes pierced their noses, the Nez Percé did not, but the name stuck. They called themselves Ne-Mee-Poo or Nimi'ipuu, which means "real people." The Kootenai (sometimes spelled *Kutenai*) and Coeur d'Alene also lived in northern Idaho.

The Shoshone, Bannock, and Paiute lived in southern Idaho. The Shoshone were the largest group in southern Idaho. They called themselves Nimi, which means "the people" or "us." Individual bands, or groups, of Shoshone also called themselves by the food they ate or the places they lived. One band that lived along the Snake River was named Kammedeka, which means "eaters of jackrabbits."

Even though the Nez Percé and the Shoshone lived hundreds of miles apart, they shared similar lifestyles. They traveled in small bands as the seasons changed to find food and survive the winters. The men hunted deer and buffalo, and fished for salmon and trout. The women grew corn, cared for children, cooked, and gathered nuts, berries, and roots to eat. Many tribes lived in teepees made of animal skins and tree branches. Others lived in homes carved out of the hillsides or built small huts.

Spirituality was important to both tribes. The Nez Percé believed that all animals and even natural forces, such as the wind and rain, had spirits. The Shoshone had great respect for animals because they believed that animals created the world for humans. When they killed animals, they used every part. They ate the meat, made clothing and shelter from the hide, and even carved tools from the bones.

Horses changed the lives of many Native Americans.

Their way of life changed when a few Native Americans in the southwest bought horses from early Spanish explorers. By the mid-1700s, tribes in Idaho that had never seen a Spaniard began trading horses with one another. The Nez Percé and Shoshone quickly became excellent horse riders and breeders. With horses, they could travel

FIND OUT MORE

The Nez Percé bred a fast and sturdy horse they named the Appaloosa. Research the Appaloosa and draw a diagram or write a report showing why it was an ideal horse for the Nez Percé.

great distances to find food. The Shoshone hunted buffalo on the Wyoming Plain, while the Nez Percé hunted for food as far away as Montana.

Horses also made it easier for Native American groups to communicate. Before horses arrived, the Nez Percé tribe was made up of many small bands. The bands were not united, and they had no overall chief. With horses, members of different bands could travel from far away to meet and choose a leader. Horses also made it possible for people from different tribes to meet every summer to trade, talk, and dance together.

EARLY EXPLORERS

About eight thousand Native Americans lived in Idaho when the first American explorers arrived in 1805. Two years earlier, the United States had purchased a huge tract of land from France. Called the Louisiana Territory, it extended west of the Mississippi River to Idaho. This exchange is called the Louisiana Purchase, and it doubled the size of the United States.

President Thomas Jefferson was eager to explore the uncharted West. He hired two men, Meriwether Lewis and William Clark, to explore the new territory and find a route to the Pacific Ocean. In the spring of 1804, Lewis and Clark gathered together about thirty-one men, two horses, and a dog, and set out from St. Louis, Missouri. The following year, they became the first Americans to reach what is now Idaho.

The explorers might have been captured or killed without the help of a nineteen-year-old Shoshone woman named Sacagawea. In 1804, Lewis and Clark hired Sacagawea's husband, a French-Canadian fur trapper named Toussaint Charbonneau, to serve as an interpreter for their expedition. Sacagawea accompanied the group.

Lewis and Clark meet the Shoshone for the first time.

Sacagawea (c.1786–1812) was probably a member of the Agaiduka, or Salmon Eater, band of Shoshone. When she was fourteen years old, an enemy tribe captured and enslaved her. Later, a French-Canadian fur trapper named Toussaint Charbonneau bought her and made her his wife. When Sacagawea and her husband joined Lewis and Clark, she quickly became a valued member of the expedition. Today, many landmarks, monuments, and memorials have been named in Sacagawea's honor. A gold U.S. dollar coin was also created to commemorate her.

She helped Lewis and Clark to identify landmarks, and to negotiate with Native American tribes in Idaho and other places who were suspicious of the white explorers. Because of her presence, the Nez Percé welcomed the explorers, and even prepared a feast of buffalo and salmon for them. In return, the explorers gave them gifts such as tobacco and cloth.

Lewis and Clark sent reports to President Jefferson about the Northwest. They told about the Native Americans they encountered, as well as the area's abundant animal and plant life. It wasn't long before adventurous fur trappers and traders came to the region to trade with Native Americans. The furs of beavers, otters, and other fur-bearing animals were used to make fashionable hats and coats, which were popular in the United States and Europe. Merchants bought about 100,000 beaver pelts every year to meet the demand.

British-Canadian trapper and explorer David Thompson set up the first trading post in 1809 on the shore of Lake Pend Oreille. In 1810,

Andrew Henry of the Missouri Fur Company established a trading camp on the Snake River. Nathaniel Wyeth built a trading post in Pocatello, Idaho, in 1834 and named it Fort Hall.

MISSIONARIES AND MINERS

Missionaries were the next group of people to arrive. They came to convert Native Americans to Christianity. Eliza and Henry Spalding founded a Presbyterian mission at Lapwai near present-day Lewiston. They built a sawmill, a flour mill, a church, and a school. They even set

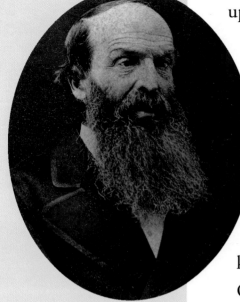

Henry Spalding was a missionary to the Nez Percé.

up a printing press. The Jesuits established the Mission of the Sacred Heart on the St. Joe River in 1842.

The missionaries tried to change the natives' ways. They wanted Native Americans to settle down and become farmers. They also told them not to worship the spirits they had honored for generations.

Most Native Americans, however, were hostile to the missionaries and refused to change their way of life. The Spaldings abandoned their mission after Native Americans in Washington killed fellow missionaries Marcus and Narcissa Whitman in 1847.

One of the most successful missionaries was Brigham Young. He led his followers, called Mormons, out of Illinois in 1848 and settled in Salt Lake City, Utah. By the mid 1850s, Mormons had also become a strong presence in southern Idaho. In 1860, they founded Idaho's first permanent settlement at Franklin.

FIND OUT MORE

Many people began migrating west in the mid-1800s. Most settlers followed the same path across the Rocky Mountains, known as the Oregon Trail. It was the first "highway" through Idaho. Thousands of Americans crossed the trail in covered wagons as it followed the Snake River across Idaho. The journey wasn't easy. They had to survive illness, accidents, the Rocky Mountains, buffalo stampedes, and violent storms. Find out more about the trail and draw a map of it from beginning to end.

In the 1800s, both Britain and the United States claimed the Northwest, including Idaho. In 1846, they reached an agreement. They divided the region into two parts at what is now the border between Canada and the United States. (At that time, Canada was controlled by the British.) Great Britain took the northern half, and the United States took the southern half. As a result, Idaho became part of the Oregon Territory, which included what is now Oregon, Washington, and part of Canada. When Oregon became a state in 1859, all of what is now Idaho became part of Washington Territory.

Few people settled there until 1860, when Elias Pierce struck gold on Orofino Creek. Thousands of people came to Idaho from all over the world hoping to get rich quick. Towns such as Placerville, Idaho City, and Pioneerville sprang up almost overnight.

By 1863, there were enough people living in the region to create a separate territory. In March 1863, the United States government carved out a new territory and named it Idaho. United States

Advertisements like these lured many people to Idaho in hopes of striking it rich.

senators chose the name over "Shoshone" and "Montana." They believed *Idaho* was a Shoshone word meaning "gem of the mountains." In fact, a steamboat operator had invented the name. Boise became the official capital of the Idaho territory in 1864.

Although they had created this new territory, Congress did not write any laws to help govern it. The territory was such a remote wilderness that, often, territorial governors never even showed up. Those who did sometimes stayed only a few months.

Without any laws, Idaho soon became a dangerous place. Roving bands of outlaws terrorized the countryside. Some settlers piled sacks of flour or sand around their beds to protect themselves from stray bullets while they slept.

NATIVE AMERICAN WARS

With so many new settlers moving into Idaho, there was little room left for Native Americans. Little by little they were forced off their land to make way for new arrivals.

In the 1850s, the United States government began negotiating treaties, or agreements, with Native Americans. The treaties forced them to live in small areas called reservations, which were set aside for their use. Many tribes refused to accept the treaties. They didn't want to abandon their homes and give up their way of life. In an effort to defend their land, they sometimes attacked the settlers. The United States Army set up Fort Boise to protect the mining camps from Native American attacks.

In 1855, the Nez Percé signed a treaty with the United States government that forced the tribe to live on two reservations: one in Idaho and one in Oregon. Many agreed because the land included much of their original territory. In 1863, after the gold rush, the United States government forced the Nez Percé to sign another treaty. This treaty greatly reduced the size of the Lapwai Reservation in Idaho.

On reservations like Lapwai, Native Americans could no longer hunt and fish as they had for generations. They had to live in square houses, instead of their round teepees. They tried to be farmers, but the soil was not good enough to grow much food.

Several Nez Percé chiefs who had not signed the treaty refused to accept it. In 1877, the United States government told Chief Joseph, leader of the Nez Percé in Wallowa Valley, Oregon, that his band must

Fort Lapwai, in the Lapwai Valley, was originally constructed to prevent whites from settling on Nez Percé land. These efforts were soon abandoned.

move to the already overcrowded Lapwai Reservation. The Nez Percé were devastated, and several young Nez Percé killed four white settlers in anger.

Chief Joseph feared the United States Army would strike back. Before soldiers arrived, he led nearly eight hundred Nez Percé, including women, children, and the elderly, on an escape route to Canada. Meanwhile two thousand United States soldiers chased them.

The Nez Percé traveled more than 1,000 miles (1,609 km) in the dead of winter before being captured on October 5, 1877, at Bears Paw Mountain in Montana. They were only 40 miles (64 km) from the

The Nez Percé fled from the U.S. Army along a route to Canada, now called the Nez Percé National Historic Trail.

Canadian border. When forced to surrender, Chief Joseph told his tribe. "My heart is sick and sad. Hear me my chiefs! From where the sun now stands, I will fight no more forever."

In 1878, the Bannock tribe also fought the United States government. For many years, the Bannock had been confined to a reservation in southern Idaho. In a treaty, the government agreed to provide food, but never did. When starving tribesmen left to hunt for food, nearby farmers grew alarmed and attacked the Bannock. Their leader, Chief Buffalo Horn, and about 140 other Bannock were killed.

Today, about 3,000 Nez Percé live on the 90,000-acre (36,422-hectare) Lapwai reservation in Idaho. Several thousand Bannock live on the Fort Hall Reservation in southeastern Idaho.

WHO'S WHO IN IDAHO?

Chief Joseph's (1840–1904) Native American name was In-mut-too-yah-lat-lat, which means "thunder rolling in the mountains." He never stopped campaigning to return his people to the Wallowa Valley, traveling the country speaking to Congress and even President Rutherford B. Hayes. In 1883, a small group of Nez Percé returned to the Wallowa Valley, but Chief Joseph was not allowed to accompany them. He died on the Colville Reservation in Washington on September 21, 1904.

EARLY STATEHOOD

On July 3, 1890, Idaho officially became the forty-third state. The state elected George Shoup, the last territorial governor, as its first governor. Boise was named the capital.

The rugged landscape of Idaho was dotted with mining operations.

The future looked bright for the new state. Gold and silver had recently been discovered in the Wood River Valley and the Coeur d'Alene River Valley, and the mining industry was booming. Businessmen built hundreds of miles of railroad tracks across the Panhandle and the Snake River Plain. They shipped millions of dollars worth of gold, silver, animals, and wool from Idaho to faraway markets.

The railroads also brought thousands of settlers to Idaho from all over the world. These immigrants played a big part in building the new state. People from China and Japan worked in Idaho's mining camps, railroads, and lumberyards. By 1870, the majority of Idaho miners were Chinese.

Although the mines brought both money and people into the new state, they also caused problems. The mines were profitable for mine owners, but the miners themselves made little money, even though they worked long hours. Miners in Idaho faced a hard life. Their jobs were dangerous. Mines could collapse or explode at any time without warning. Although mine owners were well aware of these dangers, they did nothing to improve working conditions for miners.

Violent disputes broke out at mining camps between mine owners and mine workers. To fight for better wages, the miners formed a group called a union. They named it the Western Federation of Miners. The union allowed the miners to come together and fight for their cause as an organized group. However, mine owners ignored their protests, cutting wages and firing union workers instead.

In 1892, union miners in the Coeur d'Alene region decided to stop working, or go on strike. They also fired guns at guards and exploded a pipe with dynamite. Governor Willey brought in United States Army troops to help break the strike, and many union workers hated Willey for it. This incident touched off years of tension between union members, mine owners, and government officials. In 1905, a union miner named Harry Orchard killed Frank Steunenberg, who had served as governor from 1897 to 1901. Steunenberg had also been involved in mining disputes. The murder trial that followed brought worldwide attention. Orchard went to prison, where he wrote several books about his life.

In 1892, angry miners used dynamite to destroy the Helena-Frisco mill. Mine owners considered it an act of war.

WHAT'S IN A NAME?

The names of some places in Idaho have interesting origins.

Name	Comes From or Means
Boise	Named for the Boise River, which is French for "wooded river"
Coeur d'Alene	French for "heart-of-the-awl"
Nampa	Named for Paiute chief Nampuh
Nez Percé	French for "pierced nose"
Pocatello	Named for Shoshone chief

In the 1900s, new technology helped turn Idaho into an agricultural powerhouse. Dams and canals were built on Idaho's rivers to funnel water to the dry plains. The 348-foot (106-m) Arrowrock Dam on the Boise River was the tallest in the world until 1934.

Ira Perrine built a 65-mile (105-km) canal system on the Middle Snake River. The canal turned thousands of acres of desert into fertile farmland, and Idaho's potato farmers rejoiced. The additional water and Idaho's volcanic soil helped make the state famous for its hardy Russet potatoes.

Moses Alexander, Idaho's governor from 1915 to 1919, encouraged many of these advances. He was the first Jewish person elected as governor in any state. Alexander started a highway-building plan because not even a wagon road connected northern and southern Idaho. Alexander also won higher wages and shorter workdays for Idaho's workers.

Towns like Lewiston and Potlach prospered by logging Idaho's enormous stands of forests. But that work, too, was dangerous. In 1910, a terrible fire swept through Idaho's forests, killing eighty-five people. Most who died were firefighters battling the blaze with shovels and axes. Driven by high winds and dry conditions, the fire scorched 1.7 million acres (688,000 ha) in Idaho. Despite such tragedies, Idaho tripled its timber production by 1914.

Idaho farmers continued to prosper throughout the early years of the new century. The demand for food increased during World War I (1914–1918). The United States joined the war in 1917 to help the British and the French fight against Germany and Austia-Hungary. Idaho farmers supported the war effort by supplying food to troops in Europe.

After the war ended, however, food prices plunged because demand decreased. Many farmers had taken out loans that they could not repay. As a result, many farmers lost their farms.

(opposite)
Arrowrock Dam provides much of the irrigation water for the Boise area.

Things got worse in 1929 when the stock market crashed and the Great Depression (1929–1939) hit. The depression was a time of financial hardship that affected the entire United States, and even the world. Two of Idaho's profitable industries—mining and lumbering—also lost money, as the prices of timber and silver plummeted. To make matters worse, severe droughts, or long periods of dry weather, devastated Idaho's farms in the 1930s. Much of the soil on Idaho's southern plains dried up and blew away. Very few crops would grow. Idaho became part of a region known as the "Dust Bowl" because a thin layer of powdery dust covered everything.

Many dried-up farms in Idaho were abandoned in the 1930s.

The Great Depression came to an end with the start of World War II (1939–1945). The United States entered the war on December 8, 1941, after Japan bombed Pearl Harbor, a United States naval base in Hawaii. The United States joined France, Great Britain, and their allies, or friends, in the fight against Japan, Germany, and other countries.

The war created new demand for manufactured products and food. Many people in Idaho found work in factories that made airplanes, guns, and other military supplies. Idaho's farmers could once again earn money by supplying food to soldiers fighting overseas. Demand for Idaho's timber also skyrocketed.

Important military bases were constructed in Idaho, including a naval training station at Lake Pend Oreille and air bases at Boise, Pocatello, and Mountain Home. These bases employed thousands of young men.

Not everyone prospered, however. After Japanese aircraft attacked Pearl Harbor, some officials in the United States government became suspicious of Japanese Americans. The government worried that these people might be spies, and believed that they might try to help Japan fight against the United States. Although there was no evidence of this, in 1942 the federal government rounded up thousands of Japanese Americans and sent them to internment camps.

Japanese-Americans were sent to an assembly center in Idaho.

FAMOUS FIRSTS

- Idaho was the first state to elect a Jewish governor, Moses Alexander, in 1914.
- The world's first ski chairlift was built in Sun Valley in 1936.
- The world's first nuclear power plant was built near the town of Arco in 1949.
- Idaho was the first state to ratify the Equal Rights Amendment in 1972.
- Larry EchoHawk became the first Native American to be elected as a state attorney general of Idaho in 1990.

About ten thousand Japanese Americans were sent to the Minidoka Camp near Minidoka, Idaho. Many lost their homes and possessions. When they were released in 1945, thousands stayed in Idaho. In 1988, the United States government issued an apology to the many Japanese Americans who lost liberties as a result of their incarceration. Each Japanese American who had been sent to the camps was awarded $20,000.

RECENT HISTORY

In 1949, the United States Atomic Energy Commission set up a National Reactor Testing Station near the town of Arco. It was the world's first electricity-producing nuclear power plant. In 1955, Arco became the first community in the world lighted by nuclear power.

At first, many welcomed the plant because it created thousands of jobs and brought more people to the region. Later, people learned that dangerous gases had leaked from the plant. Now called the Idaho National Engineering and Environmental Laboratory (INEEL), it currently performs research related to nuclear energy. The site is now being cleaned up, but some people worry that waste from the plant could permanently pollute the Snake River.

Many Idahoans have mixed feelings about INEEL, which now does energy-related research.

In the 1960s and 1970s, manufacturing replaced farming as Idaho's most important industry. However, most of these businesses are related to agriculture, processing food grown on Idaho's farms. More and more people began moving to cities and towns looking for work. By 1960, half the people in Idaho lived in cities or towns.

Tourism also increased as more people from all over the world began discovering the natural beauty of Idaho. By 1980, Congress had designated some 4 million acres (1.6 million ha) of Idaho land as wilderness area. That means the land is closed to any motorized vehicles. Sun Valley, a mountain ski resort, attracts thousands of tourists every year.

At the same time, the price of silver and timber dropped, causing many loggers and miners to lose their jobs. By the 1990s, the mines in Silver Valley had shut down, and the sawmills had closed for good in Potlatch, Coeur d'Alene, and other timber communities.

Clear-cutting, or cutting down large areas of trees, deprives wildlife of their habitat. However, the lumber industry provides many jobs for Idahoans.

One of the most important issues facing Idaho today is how to best use the state's wilderness areas. Some people want to open up part of the wilderness land to logging and mining to create jobs. Others say that preserving the wilderness land is important for the environment and the people of Idaho. They say that destroying Idaho's unspoiled wilderness would hurt the state's multimillion-dollar tourism industry, which depends on the region's natural beauty. Deciding how best to use the state's abundant natural resources is a debate that will shape the state's history for years to come.

CHAPTER FOUR

GOVERNING IDAHO

The capitol, completed in 1920, is Idaho's most treasured building.

Idaho became a state in 1890. Idaho is still governed under its original constitution, which was adopted in 1889. A constitution is an official document that defines the way in which a government will be run.

Idaho's constitution has been amended, or changed, more than one hundred times. However, amending the constitution isn't easy. All amendments (changes) must be approved by a two-thirds majority vote of both houses in the legislative branch—the senate and the house of representatives.

The constitution divides state government into three parts, or branches: legislative, executive, and judicial. The legislative branch makes laws; the executive branch enforces laws; and the judicial branch interprets, or explains, the laws. No one branch has more power than another. They all work together to govern Idaho.

LEGISLATIVE BRANCH

Members of the legislative branch make the state's laws. Idaho's legislature is made up of two parts, called houses: the senate and the house of representatives. The people of Idaho elect thirty-five senators and seventy representatives to serve two-year terms. Idaho is divided into thirty-five legislative areas, or districts. Each district elects one senator and two representatives. Both senators and representatives can be re-elected up to four times.

The written proposal for a new law is called a bill. The idea for a bill begins in either the senate or the house of representatives. After careful research, the bill is voted on by both houses of the legislature. If a majority of legislators vote in favor of the bill, it is passed to the governor for his or her signature. New laws may apply to education, finance, and local government, among other things. The state legislature is also responsible for creating a budget, which is a plan for spending the state's money. The money must be divided among schools, roads, and other things the state needs.

Senators discuss new laws inside the senate chambers.

The state legislature meets every year. Sessions begin the Monday on or nearest January 9 and last about 90 days. The governor may also call special legislative sessions if necessary.

EXECUTIVE BRANCH

The executive branch makes sure that state laws are carried out and enforced. The governor is head of the executive branch. The people of Idaho elect the governor, who serves a four-year term and may be re-elected only once.

The governor plays an important role in making and carrying out laws. After a bill is passed by the legislative branch, the governor either

Residents of Boise enjoy city life just minutes away from outdoor recreation.

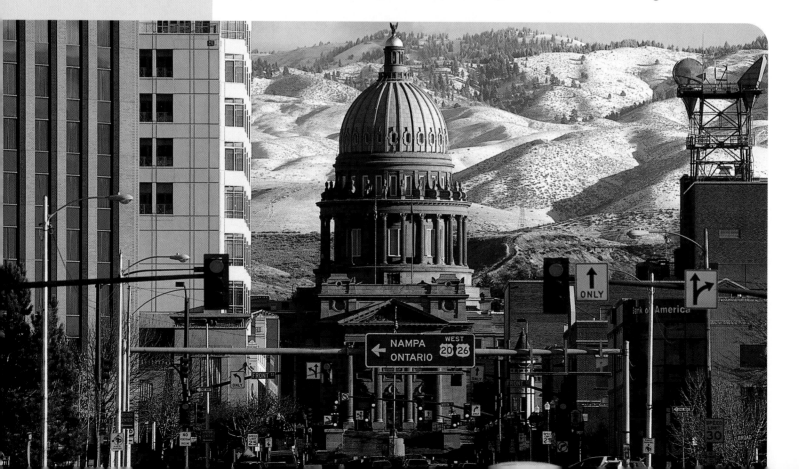

signs and approves the bill, or vetoes it, which means that he or she refuses to sign the bill into law. (However, a bill can still become a law if a majority of the legislature votes to override, or dismiss, the governor's veto.) The governor also helps the legislature decide how to spend the state's money, and acts as head of the state militia, or military forces.

The governor does not work alone. Other members of the executive branch, including the lieutenant governor, secretary of state, attorney general, controller, treasurer, and superintendent of public instruction, assist the governor. These officials are elected to four-year terms. The governor also oversees many departments in the executive branch, such as the departments of agriculture, education, and transportation.

JUDICIAL BRANCH

The judicial branch interprets, or explains, Idaho's laws and resolves disagreements about laws. There are four levels of state courts: the magistrate division, district courts, the court of appeals, and the Idaho Supreme Court.

The first level is the magistrate division. Magistrate judges hear cases regarding less serious criminal matters, called misdemeanors. A criminal case involves the breaking of a law. Magistrate judges also hear minor civil cases, or those in which two or more people are in dispute over the meaning of a law. In addition, magistrate judges hear cases relating to traffic tickets or divorce proceedings, among other things.

IDAHO STATE GOVERNMENT

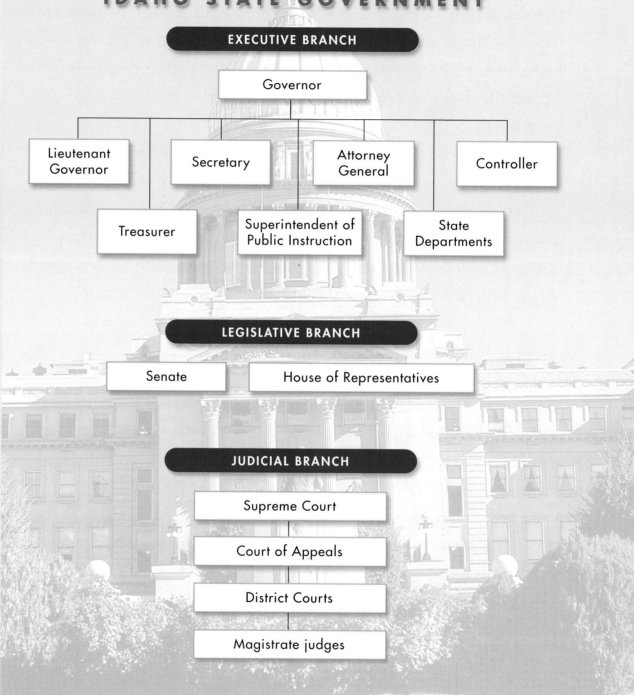

EXECUTIVE BRANCH

Governor

Lieutenant Governor

Secretary

Attorney General

Controller

Treasurer

Superintendent of Public Instruction

State Departments

LEGISLATIVE BRANCH

Senate

House of Representatives

JUDICIAL BRANCH

Supreme Court

Court of Appeals

District Courts

Magistrate judges

IDAHO GOVERNORS

Name	Term	Name	Term
George L. Shoup	1890	Barzilla W. Clark	1937–1939
N. B. Willey	1890–1893	C. A. Bottolfsen	1939–1941
William J. McConnell	1893–1897	Chase A. Clark	1941–1943
Frank Steunenberg	1897–1901	C. A. Bottolfsen	1943–1945
Frank W. Hunt	1901–1903	Chas C. Gossett	1945
John T. Morrison	1903–1905	Arnold Williams	1945–1947
Frank R. Gooding	1905–1909	C. A. Robbins	1947–1951
James H. Brady	1909–1911	Len B. Jordan	1951–1955
James H. Hawley	1911–1913	Robert E. Smylie	1955–1967
John M. Haines	1913–1915	Don Samuelson	1967–1971
Moses Alexander	1915–1919	Cecil Andrus	1971–1977
D. W. Davis	1919–1923	John V. Evans	1977–1987
Charles C. Moore	1923–1927	Cecil Andrus	1987–1995
H. C. Baldridge	1927–1931	Phillip E. Batt	1995–1999
C. Ben Ross	1931–1937	Dirk Kempthorne	1999–

Some cases begin in district court. District courts hear more serious criminal and civil cases. Idaho has seven judicial districts. Each district elects district court judges who serve four-year terms.

The court of appeals is at the next level. This court hears appeals from lower courts. If a person is not satisfied with the outcome of their case in a lower court, they may request an appeal, or a review of the case by a higher court. Judges in Idaho's court of appeals are elected to six-year terms.

Idaho's highest court is the state supreme court. This court makes the final decision on all civil and criminal appeals. It is made up of one chief justice (judge) and four associate justices. The court elects one of its members to serve as chief justice for four years. Associate justices are elected to six-year terms.

TAKE A TOUR OF BOISE, THE STATE CAPITAL

Idaho's state's capital and largest city is Boise. It lies in the southwestern part of Idaho, along the Boise River. It was named for the Boise River, which early nineteenth-century French fur traders named *Riviere Boisiere,* the French words for "wooded river." Boise has so many trees, such as cottonwoods, birches, and willows, that people call it the City of Trees.

Almost 186,000 people live in Boise. Many of these people work for the federal, state, or local government. Boise is the political heart of Idaho. The Idaho state legislature meets in the capitol building, which was completed in 1920. It is designed to look like the United States Capitol in Washington, D.C., and features a 208-foot (63-m) dome. On top of the dome sits a human-sized copper eagle. Marble from Alaska, Georgia, Vermont, and Italy lines the building's interior.

The Boise Depot was once known as the Union Pacific Railroad Depot.

From the front steps of the capitol, you can see the Boise Depot, built in 1924. It once served as the hub of Idaho rail passenger traffic. Today, the depot is a museum featuring the history of the railroad. Three blocks south of the capitol is Old Boise, the city's original downtown. The oldest building there, the Perrault-Fritchman Building, was built in 1879 of local sandstone.

Next, head east and visit the U.S. Assay Office. This cone-shaped building once processed $75 million in gold and silver ore before it closed in 1933. South of Broadway Avenue is Boise State University, Idaho's largest center of higher learning. Several footbridges link it with Julia Davis Park, the cultural heart of Boise.

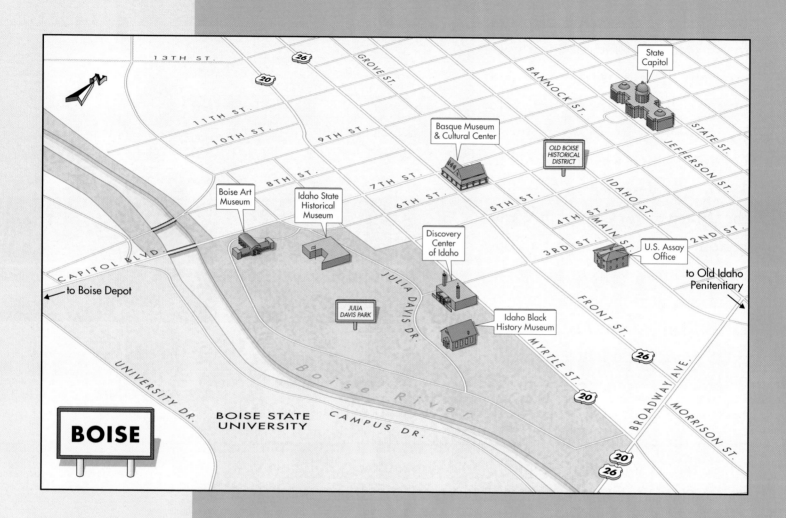

13TH ST.

GROVE ST.

BANNOCK ST.

State Capitol

11TH ST.

10TH ST.

9TH ST.

Basque Museum & Cultural Center

OLD BOISE HISTORICAL DISTRICT

STATE ST.

JEFFERSON ST.

8TH ST.

7TH ST.

Boise Art Museum

Idaho State Historical Museum

6TH ST.

5TH ST.

IDAHO ST.

4TH ST.

3RD ST.

2ND ST.

Discovery Center of Idaho

U.S. Assay Office

MAIN ST.

CAPITOL BLVD.

JULIA DAVIS DR.

to Old Idaho Penitentiary

to Boise Depot

JULIA DAVIS PARK

Idaho Black History Museum

FRONT ST.

MYRTLE ST.

UNIVERSITY DR.

BOISE STATE UNIVERSITY

CAMPUS DR.

Boise River

BROADWAY AVE.

MORRISON ST.

BOISE

At the Idaho Historical Museum, discover Idaho's history, from its fossil past to the growth of urban Boise. The Idaho Black History Museum tells about the important role of African-Americans in settling the west.

The Boise Art Museum has one of the nation's most respected collections of American art. The museum also offers artist presentations, art classes, and the art experience gallery, where children can participate in a variety of fun activities to learn how art is made. For more hands-on fun, visit the Discovery Center of Idaho. This science museum has more than one hundred exhibits about electricity, motion, and other sciences. For something different, check out Zoo Boise, which houses many animals that are native to Idaho. You can also see elk, moose, sheep, and exotic animals such as ring-tailed lemurs.

Head southeast from the park about 2 miles (3 km) and visit the Old Idaho Penitentiary. Convicts built the prison of hand-cut stone in 1870, and more than 13,000 inmates were held inside its walls. Today, it is a series of several museums where you can tour old prison cells.

South of Main Street in downtown Boise is the Grove, a public plaza and pedestrian mall where live bands sometimes play. A block west of

The Boise Art Museum hosts many art-related events for the Boise community.

SPECIAL LANGUAGE

The Basque language is called *Euskara*. No one is sure of its origins because it is very different from the languages in neighboring countries. Below are some basic English words and their translation to Euskara.

English	Euskara
Thank you	Eskerrik asko
Mother	Ama
Father	Aita
Water	Ur
Bread	Ogi

the Grove, between Capitol Boulevard and Sixth Street, is Boise's Basque Block. The Basques were sheepherders who first came to North America from the mountainous border between Spain and France in the late nineteenth century. The Basque Museum and Cultural Center display tells the story of their history, culture, and language.

There's also plenty of outdoor fun in Boise. Starting in 1968, city leaders cleaned up the Boise River and created 19 miles (31 km) of riverfront parks. Today, the river is one of Boise's biggest attractions. Every summer, more than 250,000 "river rats" escape the heat by floating along the river in rafts and inner tubes.

A group of Basque dancers celebrate their heritage at the Basque Museum and Cultural Center.

CHAPTER FIVE

THE PEOPLE AND PLACES OF IDAHO

According to the 2000 Census, about 1.3 million people make their home in Idaho, and the population is still growing. In the past ten years, the population has increased by about 400,000.

There's plenty of space for all these people. Idaho has a lot of open space, as well as big cities. The state's largest cities, such as Idaho Falls, Twin Falls, and Pocatello, are all located within 50 miles (80 km) of the Snake River Plain in southern Idaho.

Each October, residents of Ketchum participate in the Trailing of the Sheep Festival, when herds of sheep make their way to winter grazing areas.

MEET THE PEOPLE

About 9 in 10 people who live in Idaho are of European descent. Almost 1 in 100 is Asian, and another 1 in 100 is Native American. Only about five thousand African-Americans live in Idaho.

FIND OUT MORE

In the 1500s, nearly everyone in Idaho was Native American. Today, only 1 percent of the state's population is Native American. Trace the decline in Idaho's Native American population over the last six hundred years. Create a graph that illustrates your findings.

Idaho has a growing Latino population. More than one hundred thousand people from a Spanish-speaking background live in Idaho. Each year the Idaho Hispanic Youth Symposium in Sun Valley attracts three hundred students to discuss issues that are important to them.

More than eighty thousand people of Basque origin live in Idaho. The Basque people came to Idaho in the 1800s from the Basque region of France and Spain where they herded sheep in the Pyrenee Mountains. Today, Boise has the largest Basque population outside of Europe.

Education is important to the people of Idaho. There are many colleges and universities in the state, including the University of Idaho in Moscow, Idaho State University in Pocatello, and Boise State University. Many small two-year community colleges are also located throughout the state.

Almost 10,000 students attend classes at the University of Idaho.

WORKING IN IDAHO

Idaho's economy—the exchange and trade of goods and services—depends upon the state's abundant natural resources. Its soil is fertile, and Idaho has many rivers that provide low-cost electricity and irrigation. Today, Idaho is an agricultural powerhouse. Idaho grows more potatoes than any other state. Farmers also grow sugar beets, beans, wheat, and peas.

Farmers in the plains also raise beef cattle. Dairy farms can be found along the Snake River Valley. Sheep graze in the valleys and plains. Idaho also has another type of farming, called aquaculture. Aquaculture is the mass production of seafood in fish hatcheries. More trout is raised in Idaho hatcheries than in any other state.

Processing and packaging Idaho's agricultural products is also big business. Half of all the potatoes grown in Idaho are processed into dehydrated or quick-frozen products there. Beet sugar is also refined. Other places freeze or can vegetables. Many factories process meat, poultry, and wheat.

Idaho is famous for its high-quality potato crop.

Idaho is also blessed with an abundance of mineral resources. There are more than seventy-two types of precious and semiprecious stones found in the Gem State. One of the largest diamonds ever found in the United States was discovered near McCall.

Idaho raises more potatoes than any other state in the country. In fact, it is the state's most important crop. A delicious way to enjoy potatoes is in combination with another popular dish—pizza! Remember to ask an adult for help.

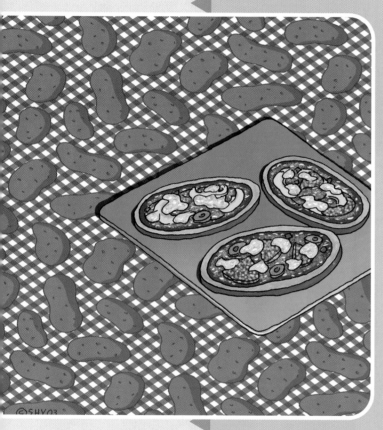

IDAHO POTATO PIZZA

Ingredients:
Vegetable oil spray
1 pound medium Idaho potatoes, scrubbed and cut
into approximately 12 1/4-inch slices
1/3 cup spaghetti sauce or bottled pizza sauce
3/4 cup shredded low fat mozzarella cheese

Options for pizza toppings:
12 slices pepperoni (quartered)
1/4 cup sliced mushrooms
1/4 cup minced green pepper
1/4 cup sliced ripe olives

1. Preheat oven to 425 degrees.
2. Spray large baking sheet with vegetable oil spray.
   Arrange potatoes on sheet in one layer; spray the potatoes.
3. Bake for 20 minutes, or until lightly browned.
4. Remove potatoes from oven. Using a spatula, turn the slices
   over on the baking sheet.
5. Spread a teaspoon of spaghetti sauce on each slice. Arrange
   desired toppings on each slice; sprinkle slices with cheese and
   bake 4 minutes until cheese is melted.
6. Using a spatula, remove slices from baking sheet and serve.
   Makes 4 servings (3 pizzas each).

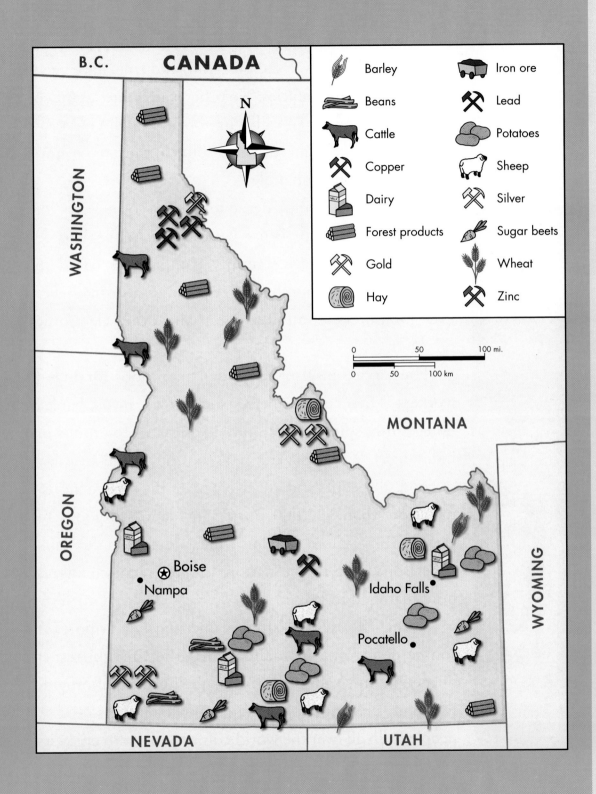

Paper mills operate in some parts of Idaho.

Minerals and metals, such as silver, copper, gold, and zinc, have been found in all of Idaho's forty-four counties. No other state mines as much silver as Idaho. Since 1884, the Silver Valley in northern Idaho has produced more than $4 billion in precious metals. Some of the largest mineral deposits lie in the northern panhandle.

Timber from Idaho's dense forests also brings in a lot of money to Idaho. Boise-Cascade, a major United States paper and office supply company, is based in Boise. A growing number of companies also manufacture computers, computer parts, and other electronic products.

The service industry provides many jobs for Idaho workers. These are businesses such as law firms, banks, hotels, or hospitals, which provide services to groups or individuals. Wholesale and retail businesses sell a variety of goods to people and are also part of the service industry. More than 120,000 people in Idaho sell goods to earn a living—more than any other industry in the state. Albertson's, one of the nation's largest retail chains, is headquartered in Boise.

In the 1950s, tourism became another important source of income in Idaho, when the first ski resort opened in Sun Valley. Tourism is the business of providing food, shelter, and entertainment for visitors. Today, people from all over the world come to Idaho to enjoy its scenic beauty. More than four million tourists come to Idaho year-round, bringing more than $1 million per year into the state.

TAKE A TOUR OF IDAHO

The Panhandle

The rugged mountains and mild climate of Idaho's panhandle make it a great place for skiers. Idaho's second-largest ski resort, the Schweitzer Mountain Resort, is located near the town of Sandpoint. There's also camping and boating at nearby Farragut State Park, which has 3 miles (5 km) of lakeshore.

For a different kind of excitement, check out Silverwood Theme Park in Athol, south of Sandpoint. This park has something for everyone, from roller coasters to bumper boats to Tiny Town, a playground for kids. You can also check out an old Victorian mining town and take a ride on the Old West Steam Train. Silverwood is the largest theme park in the Northwest—and the most fun!

Farther south is Coeur d'Alene Lake, one of the most beautiful lakes in the world. There, people can swim, fish, or

Thrill-seekers enjoy a wild ride on a roller coaster at Silverwood Theme Park.

bird-watch. The largest population of ospreys in the west live there. The Museum of Northern Idaho is in the city of Coeur d'Alene. While you're there, visit the Coeur d'Alene Indian Reservation, located just south of the lake.

Southeast of Coeur d'Alene is Cataldo, home of the Cataldo Mission. Otherwise known as the Old Mission of the Sacred Heart, it was built by Roman Catholic missionaries in the 1850s. The mission is Idaho's oldest building. Today it is part of the Old Mission State Park. Not far from Cataldo is the Wallace District Mining Museum, where photographs and other artifacts tell the history of mining in Idaho. A tour takes visitors to the nearby Sierra Silver Mine.

The Cataldo Mission was built to resemble cathedrals in Italy.

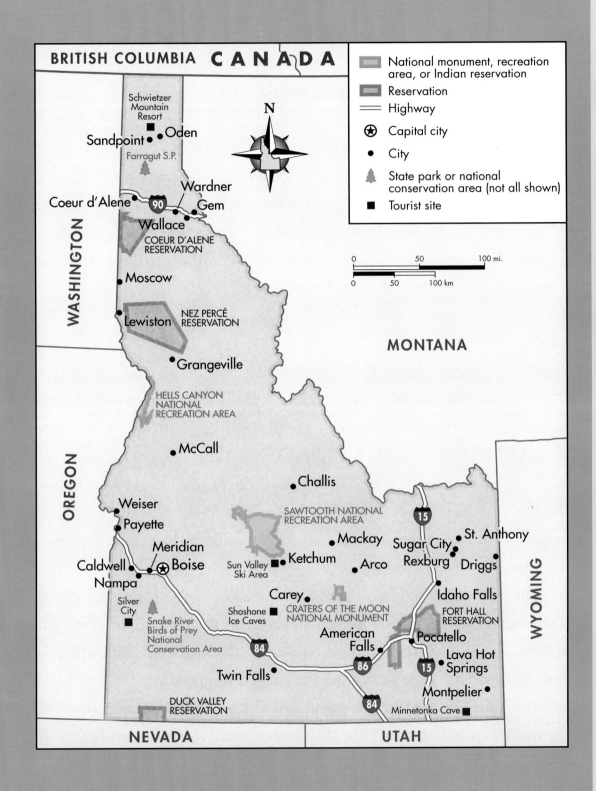

BRITISH COLUMBIA **CANADA**

N

WASHINGTON

OREGON

MONTANA

WYOMING

NEVADA UTAH

Schwietzer Mountain Resort
Sandpoint • •Oden
Farragut S.P.
Wardner
Coeur d'Alene •Gem
90
Wallace
COEUR D'ALENE RESERVATION

Moscow

Lewiston
NEZ PERCÉ RESERVATION

Grangeville

HELLS CANYON NATIONAL RECREATION AREA

McCall

Challis
SAWTOOTH NATIONAL RECREATION AREA
15
Weiser
Mackay
Sugar City •St. Anthony
Payette
Ketchum •Arco
Rexburg •Driggs
Meridian
Caldwell •Boise
Sun Valley Ski Area
Idaho Falls
Nampa
Carey
Silver City
Shoshone Ice Caves
CRATERS OF THE MOON NATIONAL MONUMENT
FORT HALL RESERVATION
Snake River Birds of Prey National Conservation Area
Pocatello
84
American Falls
86
Lava Hot Springs
15
Twin Falls
Montpelier
84
Minnetonka Cave
DUCK VALLEY RESERVATION

National monument, recreation area, or Indian reservation

Reservation

Highway

⊛ Capital city

• City

🌲 State park or national conservation area (not all shown)

■ Tourist site

0   50   100 mi.

0   50   100 km

Every April, Lewiston hosts the Dogwood Festival to showcase art from artists in Idaho, Washington, Oregon, and Montana. This colorful celebration of spring also includes a car show and a golf tournament. It all takes place under the beautiful blossoms of the area's dogwood trees.

South of Lewiston is the Nez Percé Indian Reservation. About two thousand Nez Percé still live on the reservation. Visitors can tour the Nez Percé museum to see how the tribe once lived. They can also see the Heart of the Monster, a rock formation. According to legend, blood from this rock became the Nez Percé people.

Central Idaho

Central Idaho is famous for its spectacular mountains and wild rivers. The deepest gorge in North America is at Hells Canyon National Recreation Area on the Snake River. A gorge is a deep, narrow, rocky valley, and Hells Canyon is nearly 1.5 miles (2.4 km) deep. To get the best view of the canyon, tourists hike to the top of the Seven Devil's Mountains. To the east, the Frank Church-River of No Return Wilderness Area begins. It is the largest federally protected wilderness area in the lower 48 states.

The Sawtooth National Recreation Area lies to the south and covers 1,200 square miles (3,108 sq km). The area's three hundred lakes lure fishermen, windsurfers, and water-skiers. Backpackers, hunters, and horseback riders come to explore the rugged mountains.

Sun Valley opened in 1936 and was the first winter-sports resort in North America. For only 35 cents, visitors could ride the world's first ski

A boat ride on the Snake River is one of the best ways to see Hells Canyon.

Sun Valley is a lavish ski resort nestled in central Idaho's Rocky Mountains.

lift. Nobel-Prize winning author Ernest Hemingway thrived in the natural beauty of Idaho's Sun Valley. In 1939, he wrote his famous novel, *For Whom the Bell Tolls,* at the Sun Valley Lodge.

Today, Sun Valley has more than nineteen downhill ski slopes. The resort also has four 18-hole golf courses, 85 tennis courts, riding stables, biking, swimming, hiking, and fishing. In summer, the Sun Valley Resort hosts music festivals and craft shows.

Many tourist attractions can be found near the town of Challis, such as the Custer Historic Mining town. There, visitors can see what Idaho was like when the state was a frontier wilderness. The Yankee Fork Historic Loop takes visitors to abandoned gold mines and ghost towns.

South of Boise is the Snake River Birds of Prey Natural Conservation Area. Bird-watchers can see the largest nesting place on earth for eagles, hawks, falcons, and owls. Also south of Boise is Silver City, the best-preserved ghost town in Idaho. Forty wood-frame houses and stores still stand today.

A major attraction in the Snake River Plain is the Craters of the Moon National Monument, west of Idaho Falls. Millions of years ago, lava erupted through cracks in the Earth, and today the land looks very much like the surface of the moon. It is so similar to the moon that astronauts have trained there.

Silver City was a busy mining town in the mid-1800s.

In southeast Idaho, the Twin Falls Historical Museum tells how irrigation helped agriculture grow in Idaho. Nearby observation decks at the Buzz Landon Visitors Center provide amazing views of the Snake River Canyon.

The canyon's leading attraction is Shoshone Falls, called the "Niagara of the West." At 212 feet (65 m), it is 52 feet (16 m) higher than Niagara Falls in New York. The nearby Shoshone Ice Cave is 30 feet (9.1 m) wide, 40 feet (12 m) high, and 90 feet (27 m) deep. Before refrigerators were invented, it was the only place that railroad passengers could stop for a cold drink.

Many Native American tribes participate in the Shoshone-Bannock Indian Festival each August.

In Pocatello, the Old Fort Hall recreates an 1830s trading post. The Idaho Museum of Natural History is also located in Pocatello and shows Native American artifacts, as well as the fossils of animals that roamed Idaho thousands of years ago. Every summer, the Shoshone-Bannock Indian Festival is held at the Fort Hall Indian Reservation.

Just north of Pocatello is the Shoshone-Bannock Tribal Museum on the Fort Hall Indian Reservation. About 3,000 Native Americans live on the reservation. It is one of the largest reservations in the country. Each summer, the reservation hosts the Shoshone-Bannock Indian Festival. Visitors can sample Native American foods and learn traditional Native American dances. Pocatello also hosts the annual Dodge National Circuit Finals Rodeo in March when cowboys lasso and ride bucking bulls.

Near American Falls, the Crystal Ice Cave has a frozen river, frozen waterfall, and other magnificent ice and stone formations. Some are hundreds of years old. In Idaho's southeastern corner, thousands of bats hang from the ceiling of Minnetonka Cave. Just north are the 50-million-year-old Lava Hot Springs. Each day, more than 6 million gallons (23 million liters) of steaming mineral water spew out of the springs.

The hot springs are just one of many outdoor wonders in the great state of Idaho. From waterfalls and lakes to rugged canyons and desert plains, Idaho has something for everyone. Welcome to the Gem State and its many treasures!

IDAHO ALMANAC

Statehood date and number: July 3, 1890; 43rd state

State seal: A woman holding scales and a spear symbolizes justice, liberty, and equality. A miner and a sheaf of grain stand for Idaho's farming and mineral wealth. An elk's head and a pine tree represent the state's animals and forests. Adopted in 1891.

State flag: Royal blue with gold fringe. In the center is the state seal, and below that is a scroll with the words "State of Idaho." Adopted in 1907.

Geographic center: Custer County, southwest of Challis

Total area/rank: 83,574 square miles (216,456 sq km)/13th

Borders: Montana, Wyoming, Oregon, Washington, Nevada, Utah, and Canada

Latitude and longitude: Idaho is located at approximately 42° to 49° N; 111° to 117° W

Highest/lowest elevation: Borah Peak, Custer County, 12,662 feet (3,859 m)/Snake River, Nez Percé County, 710 feet (216 m)

Hottest/coldest temperature: 118° F (48° C) on July 28, 1934, at Orofino/–60° F (–51° C) on January 18, 1943, at Island Park Dam

Land area: 82,751 square miles (214,324 sq km)

Inland water area: 823 square miles (2,132 sq km)

Population/rank (2000 Census): 1,293,953/39th

Population of major cities:

Boise: 185,787

Nampa: 51,867

Pocatella: 51,466

Idaho Falls: 50,730

Origin of state name: Name invented by George M. Willing, steamboat operator

State capital: Boise

Counties: 44

State government: 35 senators, 70 representatives

Major rivers/lakes: Snake, Salmon, Clearwater/Pend Oreille, American Falls Reservoir, Priest, Hayden, Coeur d'Alene

Farm products: Potatoes, peas, corn, sugar beets, lentils, onions, mint, barley, hops, wheat, beans, cherries, apples

Livestock: Milk cows, sheep, cattle, pigs, chickens

Manufactured products: Electronic and computer equipment, processed foods, lumber and wood products, chemical products, metals

Mining products: Phosphate rock, gold, sand and gravel, silver

Fishing products: Trout, salmon, pike, perch, crappie, bluegill

Bird: Mountain bluebird

Fish: Cutthroat trout

Flower: Syringa

Folkdance: Square dance

Fossil: Hagerman horse fossil

Gemstone: Star garnet

Horse: Appaloosa

Insect: Monarch butterfly

Motto: Esto Perpetua (Latin, meaning "Let it be perpetual")

Nicknames: Gem State, Gem of the Mountains

Song: "Here We Have Idaho"

Tree: Western white pine

Wildlife: Eagles, hawks, falcons, elk, moose, bears, deer, cougars, raccoons, otters, rabbits, foxes, skunks, squirrels

TIME**LINE**

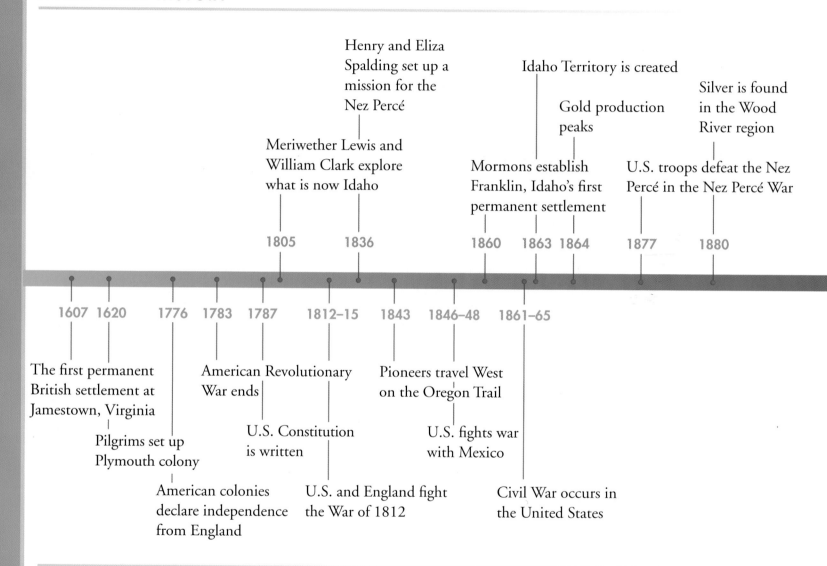

Henry and Eliza Spalding set up a mission for the Nez Percé

Idaho Territory is created

Silver is found in the Wood River region

Meriwether Lewis and William Clark explore what is now Idaho

Gold production peaks

Mormons establish Franklin, Idaho's first permanent settlement

U.S. troops defeat the Nez Percé in the Nez Percé War

1805 1836 1860 1863 1864 1877 1880

1607 1620 1776 1783 1787 1812–15 1843 1846–48 1861–65

The first permanent British settlement at Jamestown, Virginia

American Revolutionary War ends

Pioneers travel West on the Oregon Trail

Pilgrims set up Plymouth colony

U.S. Constitution is written

U.S. fights war with Mexico

American colonies declare independence from England

U.S. and England fight the War of 1812

Civil War occurs in the United States

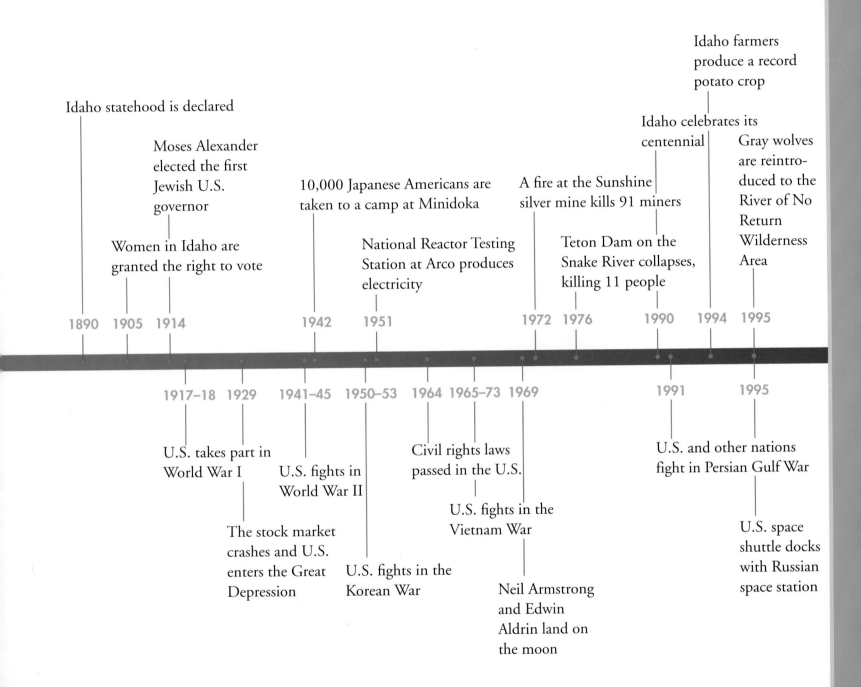

Idaho statehood is declared

Moses Alexander elected the first Jewish U.S. governor

Women in Idaho are granted the right to vote

10,000 Japanese Americans are taken to a camp at Minidoka

National Reactor Testing Station at Arco produces electricity

A fire at the Sunshine silver mine kills 91 miners

Teton Dam on the Snake River collapses, killing 11 people

Idaho farmers produce a record potato crop

Idaho celebrates its centennial

Gray wolves are reintroduced to the River of No Return Wilderness Area

1890 1905 1914   1942   1951   1972 1976   1990 1994 1995

1917–18 1929   1941–45 1950–53 1964 1965–73 1969   1991   1995

U.S. takes part in World War I

The stock market crashes and U.S. enters the Great Depression

U.S. fights in World War II

U.S. fights in the Korean War

Civil rights laws passed in the U.S.

U.S. fights in the Vietnam War

Neil Armstrong and Edwin Aldrin land on the moon

U.S. and other nations fight in Persian Gulf War

U.S. space shuttle docks with Russian space station

GALLERY OF FAMOUS IDAHOANS

Cecil Andrus

(1931–)

Served as governor of Idaho from 1971–1977 and 1987–1995. Also served as U.S. Secretary of the Interior for President Jimmy Carter. He helped create the Birds of Prey Wildlife Preserve.

Ezra Taft Benson

(1899–1994)

Served two terms as U.S. Secretary of Agriculture. He was an active member of the Mormon Church and was elected president of the Church in 1985. Born in Whitney.

Gutzon Borglum

(1867–1941)

Sculptor who was responsible for the carving of Mount Rushmore portraits of presidents Washington, Jefferson, Lincoln, and Theodore Roosevelt. Born near Bear Lake.

Carol Ryrie Brink

(1895–1981)

Children's book author. Her most well-known book is the Newbery Award-winner *Caddie Woodlawn.* Born in Moscow.

Mary Hallock Foote

(1847–1938)

Acclaimed illustrator and author of fiction about Idaho's miners and farmers. Lived near Boise.

Ernest Hemingway

(1899–1961)

Novelist who hunted and fished in Idaho. He won the Nobel Prize for literature in 1954 and is widely recognized as one of the great novelists of the twentieth century. Died in Ketchum.

Picabo Street

(1971–)

Skier and Olympic gold medalist. Born in Triumph.

Lana Turner

(1920–1995)

Popular Academy Award-winning actress. Born in Wallace.

GLOSSARY

ancient: belonging to a time long ago

canal: man-made waterway that links two bodies of water

capital: city that is the seat of government

capitol: building in which the government meets

climate: weather conditions of a region over a period of time

constitution: a document that defines the framework of a government

depression: period of widespread joblessness and poverty

drought: a prolonged period of dry weather

economy: exchange of goods and services

explorer: someone who visits and studies new lands

fossil: remains of an animal or plant that lived long ago, preserved in the Earth's crust

industry: business activity that employs many workers

legislature: branch of government that makes laws

plateau: high, level piece of land

population: number of people living in a certain location

ratify: approve

tourism: the business of providing services such as food and lodging for visitors

tributary: river that feeds a larger river or lake

wildlife refuge: place where animals are protected

FOR MORE INFORMATION

Web sites

State of Idaho Home Page
http://www.state.id.us
Everything you need to know about Idaho.

Idaho Travel and Tourism Guide
http://www.visitid.org
The best places to visit in Idaho and how to get there.

Idaho Museum of Natural History
http://www.isu.edu/departments/museum/
Learn all about the animals that roamed Idaho millions of years ago.

Idaho Department of Parks and Recreation
http://www.idahoparks.org
Learn all that Idaho's parks have to offer.

Official Nez Percé Tribal Homepage
http://www.nezperce.org
Learn about the government and history of the Nez Percé.

Books

Bial, Raymond. *The Nez Percé.* Tarrytown, NY: Benchmark Books, 2002.

Lourie, Peter. *On the Trail of Sacagawea.* Honesdale, PA: Boyds Mills Press, 2001.

O'Dell, Scott. *Thunder Rolling in the Mountains.* New York: Houghton Mifflin, 1992.

Sakurai, Gail. *Japanese American Internment Camps.* Danbury, CT: Children's Press, 2002.

Addresses

Idaho Department of Commerce
Division of Tourism Development
700 W. State Street
P. O. Box 83720
Boise, ID 83720-0093

Idaho Historical Museum
610 North Julia Davis Drive
Boise, ID 83702-7695

Office of the Governor
700 West Jefferson, 2nd Floor
P. O. Box 83720
Boise, ID 83720-0034

INDEX

ABOUT THE AUTHOR

Amy Miller is a writer and editor living in New York City. She has written articles and plays for children about many different subjects and topics. To write this book about the Gem State, she read as many books and articles as she could find.

Photographs © 2003: AP/Wide World Photos: cover (Troy Maben), 20 (Don Ryan); Archive Photos/Getty Images: 10; Brown Brothers: 39, 74 left; Buddy Mays/Travel Stock: 62; Corbis Images: 74 center right (Wally McNamee), 67 (Pierre Perrin/Sygma), 38 (Arthur Rothstein), 64 (UPI), 19 (Karl Weatherly), 36; Dave G. Houser/HouserStock, Inc./Steve Bly: 18; David R. Frazier: 3 left, 9, 17, 55, 57, 60, 65, 70 top, 71 bottom left; Dembinsky Photo Assoc.: 71 bottom right (Domonique Braud), 3 right, 66 right (Mark E. Gibson); Folio, Inc./ David R. Frazier: 45, 51; Getty Images: 13 (Laguna Photo), 74 bottom right (Swann); Hulton|Archive/Getty Images: 26, 66 left, 74 top right; Idaho State Historical Society: 41 (Argonne National Library), 28 top; MapQuest.com, Inc.: 70 center; North Wind Picture Archives: 22, 23, 27, 28 bottom, 31, 32, 34, 35; Photo Researchers, NY: 42, 46 (David R. Frazier), 71 top left (Maslowski); Steve Bly: 4, 44, 48 background, 53, 54, 56, 61, 68, 70 bottom; Steve Mulligan Photography: 14; Stock Montage, Inc.: 29; Stone/Getty Images/Tom Tracy: 21; Superstock, Inc.: 7, 25, 33; The Image Works/David Frazier: 8, 16; Tom Till Photography, Inc.: 11; Visuals Unlimited/Gerald & Buff Corsi: 71 top right.